PHOTOGRAPHIC MEMORY

*Simple, Proven Methods to Remembering
Anything Faster, Longer, Better*

© Copyright 2017 by Ryan James - All rights reserved.

The following Book is reproduced below with the goal of providing information that is as accurate and as reliable as possible. Regardless, purchasing this Book can be seen as consent to the fact that both the publisher and the author of this book are in no way experts on the topics discussed within, and that any recommendations or suggestions made herein are for entertainment purposes only. Professionals should be consulted as needed before undertaking any of the action endorsed herein.

This declaration is deemed fair and valid by both the American Bar Association and the Committee of Publishers Association and is legally binding throughout the United States.

Furthermore, the transmission, duplication or reproduction of any of the following work, including precise information, will be considered an illegal act, irrespective whether it is done electronically or in print. The legality extends to creating a secondary or tertiary copy of the work or a recorded copy and is only allowed with express written consent of the Publisher. All additional rights are reserved.

The information in the following pages is broadly considered to be a truthful and accurate account of facts, and as such any inattention, use or misuse of the information in question by the reader will render any resulting actions solely under their purview. There are no scenarios in which the publisher or the original author of this work can be in any fashion deemed liable for any hardship or damages that may befall them after undertaking information described herein.

Additionally, the information found on the following pages is intended for informational purposes only and should thus be considered, universal. As befitting its nature, the information presented is without assurance regarding its continued validity or interim quality. Trademarks that mentioned are done without written consent and can in no way be considered an endorsement from the trademark holder.

Table of Contents

Introduction 1

Chapter 1: Understanding the Memory 5

Chapter 2: Photographic Memory 9

Chapter 3: Creative Thinking 13

Chapter 4: Visualization 19

Chapter 5: Introduction to Memorization Techniques 25

Chapter 6: Peg Systems 33

Chapter 7: Emotion-based Memorization 45

Chapter 8: Mind Mapping 55

Chapter 9: Visualizing Names 65

Chapter 10: Visualizing Numbers (Major System) 75

Chapter 11: Visualizing Numbers (Other Systems) 85

Chapter 12: Memory Palace 95

Conclusion 104

INTRODUCTION

If I tell you to imagine 9,471,037,094,871 wolves flying in the sky, you'll probably picture a pack of flying wolves in your head; but will you imagine the exact number of wolves? No, you won't—bet you didn't even bother reading the numbers, did you?

Our minds find it easier to process information that has a picture of an existing object than something that is purely abstract. That is why people can remember faces more quickly than telephone numbers. After imagining the case above, you probably can still remember what kind of animals you have just imagined. However, if you will be asked, "how many wolves were there in your imagination?" You'll probably need to go back to the first paragraph before you can answer.

The reason behind such is that our minds can visualize words but not numbers. Visualization is the process of forming mental images in mind. These mental images stay in the mind longer than plain text and numbers. People associate this with the term "photographic memory." It is said to be the ability to remember a memory depicting a scene or a picture, and being able to mentally examine every detail on it.

There are a lot of things, however, beyond the term "photographic memory" that you need to know. Things about your mind that can help you clearly understand how your memory works. Things that can be the key to achieve an extraordinary retention capacity. Your memory has a lot of secrets and tricks—it's just waiting for you to discover them firsthand.

Your Free Gift

As a way of saying thanks for your purchase, I wanted to offer you a free bonus E-book called *"How to Talk to Anyone: 50 Best Tips and Tricks to Build Instant Rapport"*.

Within this comprehensive guide, you will find information on:

- How to make a killer first impression

- Tips on becoming a great listener

- Using the FORM method for asking good questions

- Developing a great body language

- How to never run out of things to say

- Bonus chapters on Persuasion, Emotional Intelligence, and How to Analyze People

To grab your free bonus book just tap here, or go to:

http://ryanjames.successpublishing.club/freebonus/

CHAPTER 1

UNDERSTANDING THE MEMORY

Memory is one of the key mental faculties. It is the mind's ability to retain and retrieve information. To understand how information is processed to become a memory, it is important to know the three main stages of memory creation: encoding, storage, and retrieval.

Encoding happens when the brain registers the stimulus that the body receives through its senses. A stimulus is basically anything that triggers the body to react or respond. Once it reaches the brain, the brain will decide whether to delete it or encode it. Attention plays an important role in this process as it determines whether the new information is going to be encoded or not. The more attention a stimulus receives, the more likely it is going to be encoded.

The storage phase is the actual process of retention. This is where the information is filtered into either short-term or long-term memory. Emotions highly influence the storage process as information with an elevated degree of emotional impact tend to be stored more in the long-term memory. The retrieval stage, on the other hand, is the process through which the mind recalls the previously stored information. It is what makes a memory an actual memory for it is where "remembering" happens.

One of the models that have greatly influenced the study of memory is the Atkinson–Shiffrin memory model, proposed by Richard Atkinson, a professor of psychology; and Richard Shiffrin, a professor of cognitive science on 1968. According to this model, a human memory is composed of three components namely, sensory register, short-term memory, and long-term memory.

Sensory Register

A sensory register—a register or stimulus received through the senses—usually does not reach the storage phase as it is easily forgotten or neglected. According to Akinson and Shiffin, the mind is prevented from receiving an overwhelming number of stimuli because a sensory register decays immediately unless it receives enough amount of attention. If it does, the brain stores it in the short-term memory.

Short-term Memory

A short-term memory, also known as a working memory, is a memory that can stay in the brain for about 18 to 30 seconds if not rehearsed. Akinson and Shiffin explained that an information is rehearsed when it is repeated over and over in one's brain. A short-term memory can further be transferred into the long-term storage of memories.

Long-term Memory

When an information is held in the short-term memory storage for a considerably long period, it is automatically transferred to the long-term memory storage; thus, it becomes a long-term memory. Traumatic and other experiences that have impacted a person emotionally are usually brought to the long-term memory store. The period of time within which a long-term memory is stored is indefinite. It can last for a year or for a lifetime and is usually lost only when the brain starts deteriorating, itself.

CHAPTER 2

PHOTOGRAPHIC MEMORY

Photographic memory is associated with the visual memory system of the brain. The mental images your brain receives through your vision of any object, is stored to the visual memory. It is also where your brain can retrieve information in the form of an image. The type of sensory register that brings visual stimulus or "icon" to the brain is called the iconic memory.

Instances like being able to visualize where exactly that answer in an exam is located on the book, or being able to imagine the sequence of all the things on a list, is commonly attributed to photographic memory. The term "photographic memory" is generally used interchangeably with the term "eidetic memory."

Eidetic Memory

Although both terms are used interchangeably, eidetic memory is not completely the same with photographic memory. Eidetic memory is the ability to recall memories in the form of images or "photographs". The visuals created under eidetic memory is vivid and accurately detailed; although there are factors which can alter it as any memory is subject to distortion. Additionally, the image is usually gone in just a matter of seconds or minutes, after the icon fades or upon interference of an action such as blinking.

So how is it different from photographic memory? Photographic memory, in contrast to eidetic memory, is the ability to recall information in a very detailed manner. It is said that if a person has a photographic memory, he can remember the exact numbers or text on a page as if the actual page is in front of the eyes.

Another thing is that photographic memory is said to be limited only to the visual memory. Eidetic memory, on the other hand, involves other senses like auditory, olfactory, and tactile. Furthermore, eidetic imagery capability has only been found in children and not in adults.

Setting Your Mind

"But I don't have a photographic memory?"

As defined above, the term "photographic memory" really seems to be an ability that is impossible to attain. It sounds like a talent that can be acquired only when you're born with it and not a skill that you can learn. Actually, there is no solid scientific evidence to this "photographic memory" that exists today. But come to think of it, what if we redefine the term "photographic memory?"

You may be starting to wonder, "how can those people with extraordinary memories remember information if they do not have a photographic memory?" Answers to that question may vary but let me emphasize the most realistic answer of all—skills.

Those people rely purely on their skills to memorize patterns and details among sets of information; thus, you call them skilled and not necessarily talented. These skills are what makes them look like they have a photographic memory. If we try to link these skills and techniques to the term "photographic memory," we can actually derive a more realistic definition for the same exact term.

Believe me, the concept of photographic memory is so near to the concepts of the most renowned memorization techniques today. These techniques have been making dramatic improvements among people's memory for centuries. And you know what makes these techniques better? It is the fact that you are about to learn these skills as you read more through the chapters. So, let us start redefining the photographic memory, and most importantly—start redefining how your own memory works.

CHAPTER 3

CREATIVE THINKING

The idea of photographic memory and the techniques that you will eventually learn are both under the same concept—creative thinking. Creative thinking is your way to meet the demands of a great memory; but what exactly is creative thinking?

Imagine you are in a zoo along with some tourists, and the tour guide introduces the following animals to you:

- Lark the zebra
- Cupid the tiger
- Red the elephant
- Nick the giraffe
- King the lion
- Orange the gorilla
- Lizzie the python
- Kurt the hippopotamus

- Bryce the ostrich

Now that they have just been introduced to you, can you recite all of their names without looking back on the list?

If you tried to but couldn't recite all of them, then it is most probably either because you just read their names or because you just said their names out loud – perhaps twice, as you think that is how your memory works. Well, it is true that repetition of an idea increases the chances of it, being retained inside your head; but the main problem with that practice is, you cannot jump into the exact position of an idea without reciting the whole list over again.

Let's say for example, without looking at the list, can you tell the name of the hippopotamus? You cannot remember it immediately, can you? Memorizing a list plainly is basically memorizing a sequence. The issue with it is that your mind needs to stick to the order of data in order to retrieve memories properly. Meaning, you cannot jump into a particular information without first reciting some or all of the information that come before it. This is where creativity needs to enter.

Creativity expands the encoding capacity of the brain. It makes the stimuli reach the storage phase by somehow forcing them to undergo an unconventional way of encoding. As you have learned in one of the previous chapters, a datum is only encoded in the brain when it is given attention otherwise it is going to decay instantly. Once encoded, the level of attention provided will dictate whether the datum is going to be stored or not. Creative methods of memorization boost the attention level that the brain can normally provide to a certain stimulus. There are a lot of basic ways you can learn to provide a solid foundation to your creative thinking but in here, we'll focus only on the three Cs: clueing, connecting, and creating.

Clueing

Let's forget about the list of those adorable animals for a while and discuss about the first C which is the clueing. If you are memorizing names, try to find something along the letters in the subject's name that you think resembles or gives a "clue" about the subject, itself. Let's take Nick the giraffe as an example. What do all giraffes have in common? A super long neck. Now, if you are going to analyze,

Nick is just one letter different from the word "neck." In this case, you have found a clue that will make you interpret Nick as neck and eventually link it to the giraffe you have just met in the zoo.

You can also use the clueing method to Lark the zebra and Kurt the hippopotamus. If you are going to replace the L with an M, Lark will turn into mark. And what distinguishes zebras from other horses? It's the presence of stripes on their skin. They have "mark"s on them. So, the zebra with marks is named Lark. On the other hand, Kurt the hippopotamus lives in the dirt. Or you can say that Kurt lives in the dirt. "Kurt" rhymes with "dirt." Therefore, if you need to remember what the hippopotamus' name is, just remember he lives in the dirt.

Connecting

The second C requires an extended and somehow, more logical reasoning. Let's use King the lion as an example. King is actually the easiest to remember since lions are labeled as kings of the jungle. But even without the term "king of the jungle," you can still easily connect the name "King" to a lion. A king is always looked up as a man of pride and coincidentally, a group of lions is called a pride. Lion is to pride, and pride is to a king; hence, the lion is King.

Lizzie, on the other hand, sounds almost like lazy. Just imagine that the python was so lazy that all it ever does is crawl the whole day and voila! You'll now be able to remember who's the Lizzie-est (laziest) of them all! The gorilla named Orange seems like hard to remember but using the connecting method, you can tie up the subject with its name. The word that will serve as a link to connect "Orange" to "gorilla," is the "orangutan." Replacing the "-utan" in orangutan with a letter E, you can get the word "Orange." Think of it as if "Orange" is a name for an orangutan. But since there was no orangutan in the zoo, the nearest alternative you'd think of is an animal that belongs to the same species—in your case, the gorilla.

Creating, the third C, will be elaborately discussed on the next chapter. It is the most flexible method which can be used to effectively encode whatever data or information you want your mind to store. Since you have learned about the first two methods, it will be easier for you to understand the idea of creating mental images or visualization. Onto the next chapter!

CHAPTER 4

VISUALIZATION

Unlike the first two methods of basic creative thinking, creating is not limited to connecting or finding a clue using the letters of the word. In fact, it does not have any limit at all. And the best thing about creating is that it does not follow formality and propriety. It doesn't even have to be realistic and logical. As long as you use your imagination, you are basically free to use this method.

The term "creating" refers to the projection or creation of a mental image in the mind by the use of imagination. For this reason, we can also call this method "visualization" which is the common term for such process. There is only one rule you need to follow when you are visualizing or creating—exaggerate.

Let's start with Cupid the tiger. Cupid does not have a general connection with the animal tiger. In this case, the only option you have is to create a visual inside your head that will make you remember "Cupid" as the name of the tiger in that zoo. So, I need you to imagine a pink-colored tiger whose fur, instead of striped, is marked with tiny red heart-shaped spots. Imagine it always flies around the forest using the pair of white feather wings on its back. It's like the famous Cupid of Valentine's Day but the difference is that it is a tiger and not a child.

The next example we have is Red the Elephant. Sure, the word "red" is so easy to remember; but can you still remember it when it is mixed with the other names? To attach the word "red" to elephant, think of a red-colored elephant that is as tiny as an ant. An elephant that is the size of an ant doesn't exist but your mind will remember it, as well as its color and name. What's the rule again? Exaggerate. If your mind can enlarge something to a size of a planet, then it can also reduce the size of something down to an atom.

For the last example, we have Bryce the ostrich. Ostrich is known to be one of those birds which cannot fly due to the unbalanced proportion between their puny wings and their heavy body weight. Imagine the utter disappointment the ostrich in that zoo felt when he found out that he couldn't fly despite being a bird. Every time he sees other birds fly, he feels so frustrated that he cries. Using the rhyming method, if an ostrich cries, then its name is Bryce.

How Visualization Sticks to the Memory

You already know that it is the attention which decides whether a stimulus is going to be encoded or not. If you are strolling around a park and you see a couple, you will probably forget about them minutes after; but if you come across a cosplayer, you'll probably spend few seconds longer looking at the details of his costume. It is more probable that you'll remember the cosplayer rather than the couple. Attention is relatively high when the brain receives uncommon stimuli. Therefore, when the body senses something strange, the stimuli immediately pass through the encoding stage and subsequently enter the storage process, even in the absence of consciousness.

Same thing happens when the brain creates mental image on its own. Visualization of a scenario that happens on a day to day basis like eating, taking a bath, and sleeping, is not necessarily retained in your memory because your mind does not generally attend to such things. But imagining impossible happenings like eating a chocolate cake that is as huge as your house, or sleeping on a bed that floats above the sea by itself, usually causes the brain to pay attention and consider encoding the stimuli.

Mental images that are unrealistic and exaggerated stick more to the memory because their oddity is easier to remember. When you retrieve a memory, your brain readies all the available pictures that can specifically satisfy what you want to remember. However, if there are a lot of pictures that look similar to what you want to remember, chances are you will get an altered or distorted memory. Similarity among memories can cause alteration of the real scene and might cause the memories to overlap. Differently, when something odd is encoded in the brain, there is no other comparable material that can cause conflict during retrieval; hence, the visual representation of the memory is more precise and is more easily remembered. Visualization might be weird and all but remember, what is out of this world is usually what stays in your mind.

Now let's go back to the list of the animals introduced by the tour guide but this time you need to fill in the blanks using your memory. See if you can remember them all:

- _____ is the name of the elephant

- Lizzie is a _____

- Orange is a _____

- _____ is the hippopotamus

- Cupid is a ____ while King is a _____

- _____ is the name of the ostrich

- The zebra's name is _____

- Nick is a _____

"Visualization takes much effort. How is it better than the method of repeating information?" Repeating the set of information over and over until retained might seem to be easier at first. But is only because you are used to memorizing things that way. You haven't tried visualization much so you think it would take more time and effort for you to imagine a scenario for every separate information. But if you use this method more frequently, you'll find out that it's actually easy. Plus, it trains your brain to be more resourceful with the available knowledge you have. It will take a lot of practice but hey, practice is the only key to an ultimate memory anyway.

CHAPTER 5

INTRODUCTION TO MEMORIZATION TECHNIQUES

From now on, the basics of creative thinking will serve as your foundation to everything that you are going to learn. So it would be best to make sure that you fully understand them. Although you don't have to worry about not yet being able to master them as you don't have to. Creative thinking takes a lot of practice and experience; therefore, so is advanced memorization techniques.

During the old ages, people did not have access to instant memorization aids. Writing a long script would just consume a large amount of ink. Cue cards were not yet widely used. Besides, assistance is not quite good for the image of any orator or speaker that time. There were no visual aids, no PowerPoint, and no other materials that would help them remember information better and faster. Thus, memorization was all about pure skill.

In order to remember massive information, people created several techniques that would help their brain retain multiple sets of data without the need of aiding materials. These people are also called "mnemonists" which is the term for individuals who possess exceptional ability to recall a number of details with ease. Since then, the invented techniques have been proven to provide dramatic results. In fact, majority of them are still being used today.

Rote Learning

Rote learning is the usual yet least favored technique of knowledge retention. It is similar to Akinson and Shiffrin's rehearsal wherein a person repeats a list of information over and over until retained in his memory. It is the least favored technique because it tends to skip the actual learning process and does not promote creativity. Unless rehearsed more frequent than usual, information encoded through rote learning usually does not last more than a day since it already starts fading in just a matter of hours. This is the reason it is used by students who cram or who memorize lessons few hours before their actual exam.

Mnemonics

Another usual technique used most especially in school is the mnemonic. This is normally used to memorize details that belong to a common group or list. Instead of memorizing the whole list, the initials or parts of the words are combined to form another word, phrase, or sentence which is easier to remember.

Linking

Rote learning and mnemonics may not require visualization; but linking, together with all the other proceeding techniques, requires one. Linking is the method of connecting adjacent details on a list. It's basically visualizing mental images that represent the connection of the first detail to the second one, the second detail to the third one, the third detail to the fourth one, and so on. To demonstrate, take note of the given short list of the first world countries below:

- United States
- Canada

- Bermuda
- Iceland
- Denmark
- Switzerland
- Ireland
- San Marino
- Norway
- Luxembourg

Using the linking method, you need to choose a visual for each of the country listed. You may start the sequence of scenarios with a picture of yourself, watching shooting stars (America's star-spangled flag) in slow motion. Next, imagine the stars that hit the ground eventually transforming into maple leaves (Canada's maple leaf). After then, the maple leaves started turning green as if they are creating a field of bermudagrass (Bermuda). Then the bermudagrass field started turning into an ice field (Iceland), and so on and so forth. Again, exaggerate the scenarios. They do not have to be realistic. And that's how simple the linking method goes. It is a good option when you want remember a list of data that follows a strict order.

Peg Systems

Peg systems are also good for data in sequence. They are one of the most effective memorization techniques as a single peg can be applied to different lists. It initially requires a preliminary list before the memorizing the actual information needed. You will learn more about the pegs in the next chapter.

Emotion-based Memorization

One of the aspect that affects the storage of an information is the emotional content. In this technique, an individual applies emotion to each information on the list. The emotion to associate with each detail should, as much as possible, be distinct from that of the other. This technique requires a deeper connection to imagination since emotions during visualization should be felt by the user as if they are real. This will be further explained on chapter 7.

Mind Map

Mind map or mind mapping is the use of a diagram to mentally organize information in mind. This method is fit for those individuals who can maintain focus while creating a detailed diagram inside their head; although the diagram can also be initially drawn on a piece of paper. Mind mapping is commonly used to memorize a whole set of related information such a lesson with topics and subtopics. This technique will be elaborated on chapter 8.

Visualizing Names

People often find issues when it comes to memorizing names. Fortunately, there is a certain technique that is developed to make remembering names easier. You'll learn about this technique on chapter 9.

Visualizing Numbers

Methods under this suggest a way to ease the difficulties on memorizing numbers. They are actually one of those peg systems but they are specifically developed to deal with numbers. They use representations to help the mind visualize numbers. The specific techniques will be demonstrated on chapters 10 and 11.

Memory Palace

Mnemonists label this technique as the most effective method of memorization. It is pretty much like creating a storage inside your head in the form of any physical object through which you can consciously retrieve information with ease. The size and complexity of the storage depends on your choice. You can make the memory storage look as simple as a cabinet or as complex as a maze. You'll find out how it works and how easy it is to learn on chapter 12.

CHAPTER 6

PEG SYSTEMS

Peg systems are a type of memorization technique wherein an individual memorizes an initial or original list of representational objects that will later be used to memorize another list of information. The objects on the initial list serve as the "pegs" of the system and each of them represents and substitutes a certain number. Thus, instead of memorizing the information by their numerical sequence, you can just assign a peg to each of them.

The initial list generally does not change and does not contain the actual information to memorize. It is like a permanent list in your mind that is meant to be associated with any other list of information and is usually made of easy-to-visualize words. This technique is commonly used to memorize a sequence of information.

There are different types of peg systems namely, the number rhyme, the number shape, the alphabet system, the major system, and the PAO system. Although similar in purpose, each of them has a different way of assigning pegs to a number of information.

Number Rhyme

From the name itself, the number rhyme uses the names of objects that rhyme with the numbers on the list. To further understand, take a look at the list below and try to memorize it:

01 - bun (as in bread roll)
02 - shoe
03 - tree
04 - boar
05 - hive (as in beehive)
06 - cheeks
07 - heaven
08 - plate
09 - sign (as in street signs)
10 - hen (as in a female bird)

The list is what we call an original list. Once pre-memorized, it can be associated with another list that contains the information you need to memorize. You may choose to assign your own pegs or just adopt the same list. It's completely up to you. Just make sure that your mind can easily picture each word since you don't want your original list to be an additional burden. But for this specific exercise, we will be using the mentioned list.

Let's say for example, you need to shop groceries but for a certain reason, you do not want to bring a grocery list. So, in order to make sure that you will not miss any item, you decided to memorize the list before going to the supermarket.

Grocery List:

- shampoo
- toothpaste
- soda in can
- apple juice
- lemons
- prunes
- tomatoes
- beef

- bell pepper
- cabbage

Now, try to associate your grocery list to the original list you have using the number rhyme peg system. The first thing on your to-buy list is shampoo while the first word on your initial list is bun. So, imagine yourself eating a bun with a shampoo filling. Yes, it's gross but remember, that is how things stick in your mind. Moving on, try to imagine yourself cleaning your white shoes with toothpaste. That shall connect "shoe" with "toothpaste." Next, think of a tree that bears sodas in can as its fruits so you can quickly remember the not-so-healthy third item. Following the rest of the list, imagine the following scenarios in sequence: a boar swimming in a pond of apple juice, a beehive that contains lemons instead of honey, your cheeks getting so wrinkled that they start looking like prunes, angels in heaven throwing tomatoes at each other while playing, a huge plate containing a meat of beef that is as large as the table, a green traffic sign in the shape of a bell pepper, and a hen sitting on her nest that is made of cabbage leaves.

You can use the original list you developed over and over again to memorize another set or list of information. That is how the number rhyme system—and generally the peg systems—is used. You don't have to force your brain to enumerate all the items on your grocery list. You just need to reimagine all the scenarios you have made in your head using the peg system.

Number Shape

01 - pen
02 - swan
03 - flying bird
04 - flag
05 – hook hand or hook
06 - golf club
07 - ramp
08 - infinity sign
09 - balloon
10 – snail

To explain how each peg is related to its corresponding number, imagine these numbers forming the shapes of the pegs. The number one is like a pen. Number two is like the curve from a swan's breast up to its bill. Three is that m-shaped bird we all have drawn when we were young. Four is like a flag with a triangular banner. Five is like a pirate's hook hand facing down. Six's shape is like a golf club. Seven is like a skateboard ramp rotated 90°. Eight is just a vertical infinity sign. Nine is like a balloon. Ten is like a snail crawling up a rock or a snail rotated 90°; its body is the number one while its shell is the zero.

Unlike number rhyme, the number shape uses the shape of the objects to substitute numbering. Again, you can change the images if you have a better replacement or something that is easier for you to imagine. Of course, you have to memorize the images first before you can memorize the information you need. Let us use the same grocery list which was cited previously on the number rhyme system as an example.

First, imagine yourself writing on a paper using a pen which uses shampoo as its ink. Second, imagine a swan living on a lake that is made up of toothpaste instead of water. Third, imagine a flying bird drinking soda in the sky. Fourth, think of a large apple with a flag on top. Fifth, imagine yourself as a pirate captain eating a lemon with your hook hand.

Sixth, picture yourself playing golf and hitting prunes that are as large as golf balls. Seventh, imagine you are a skateboarder and one of your exhibitions is skating up a ramp while juggling tomatoes. Eighth, visualize your refrigerator producing infinite number of beef every day. Ninth, imagine a bell pepper floating like a balloon up the sky. Tenth, imagine a gigantic snail whose shell is an actual cabbage.

Alphabet Peg System

If you prefer organizing the information using the letters in the English alphabet system instead of numbering them, then you can use the alphabet peg system. It works basically the same way as the previous peg systems except that you associate information with pegs that represent the letters in the alphabet. It also can only cover up to 26 pieces of information due to the limited characters of the alphabet.

There are three methods under the alphabet peg system namely, the initial letter method, the letter sound method, and the letter shape method. The original list created under the initial letter method contains objects whose names start with the corresponding letters in the alphabet. For example: axe, ball, carpet, door, egg, fork, gun, house, etc.

The letter sound method, on the other hand, uses objects whose sounds start the same as the sounds of the letters in the alphabet like "ape" for a, "bin" for b, "sea" for c, etc. The letter shape, of course, uses objects whose shapes are almost like those of the letters; so, you can imagine a ladder for A, eyeglasses rotated 90° for B, or a crescent moon for C.

Let's say for example you have to memorize the 17 basic types of psychology for an exam. Using the initial letter method, you've come up with the list below:

A - axe
B - barber
C - chicken
D - dog
E - egg
F - fireworks
G - gate
H - house
I - ink

J - juice
K - knife
L - leaf
M - moon
N - necklace
O - oven
P – phone
Q – queen

To start, imagine a man whirling his axe on the street scaring people (abnormal psychology). Then think of a barber who keeps on insulting his customers. People say his attitude is in his genes (behavioral genetics). The chicken in your neighborhood is actually a biological child of your neighbors (biological psychology); it's their son. Imagine a smart dog that talks about problem solving skills (cognitive psychology). Visualize an egg singing a European song while being boiled in its Asian-themed shell (cross-cultural psychology). Imagine the fireworks spelling out "I'm different" in the sky (differential psychology). Think of an old-looking gate that serves as a portal to a hidden cultural museum (cultural psychology). Think of a house that is under development (developmental psychology). Think of the word "evolution" written in ink (evolutionary psychology). Imagine experimenting with the different flavors of juice (experimental psychology). Imagine yourself stabbing your Math test paper with a knife because you can't answer the problems (mathematical psychology). Imagine discovering a kind of leaf that improves the functions of all your neurons (neuropsychology). Imagine the moon telling you how he likes the sun's personality (personality psychology). Visualize yourself wearing a necklace with a plus pendant (positive psychology). Think of an oven that bakes numbers (quantitative psychology). Try to compare your new phone with the first phone you had (comparative psychology). Imagine a queen who keeps on hanging out with her friends and acquaintances (social psychology).

Now try to answer the following questions without looking back to the mentioned types of psychology above:

- What type of psychology is linked to the barber who insults his customers?

- What type of psychology is associated with the chicken in your neighborhood?

- What type of psychology does the boiled egg represent?

- What type of psychology is linked to the hidden gate?

- What type of psychology does the knife represent?

- What type of psychology is associated with the necklace with a plus pendant?

- What type of psychology is linked to the queen who always hangs out with her friends?

If you answered at least four questions right, then that means you are doing great. However, if you were not able to attain four correct answers, that's fine. You can still learn and practice more techniques as you go further through the next chapters, including the other peg systems that have special and specific purposes.

CHAPTER 7

EMOTION-BASED MEMORIZATION

Can you still recall the first lesson you had in high school? Well, there's actually a high possibility that you can't. But, do you still remember your first heart break? Of course, you do. No matter how painful, saddening, or fulfilling it was, nobody forgets his first love.

Actually, the fact that your first heart break was painful, saddening, or fulfilling, is the exact reason you still remember it. Information that is charged with enough level of any emotion is more likely to be encoded and stored. As previously mentioned, emotions play an important role in the encoding phase for it heightens the level of attention designated to a certain stimulus. This means that emotions serve as a guarantee for a certain stimulus to subconsciously pass through encoding process; thus, greater probability of getting stored in the brain.

Moreover, emotions can dominate the importance of information. Long-term memory store contains more emotionally-driven memories than consciously injected information. If I tell you to remember any happy moment there will surely be one that is going to pop up in your head. But if I tell you to recite your company's or school's contact number, you won't recall it quickly or possibly, you won't recall anything at all because you simply do not have a memory of it stored in your brain. Your happy moments cannot save you in case of emergency but the school's or company's contact number can. However, your brain tends to easily retrieve those moments quickly as they are charged with feelings—happiness—unlike the contact number which needs to be rehearsed multiple times despite its importance to you.

Mood

An emotional aspect that is closely related to the functioning of memory is the mood. It is a less specific emotional state brought not necessarily by external stimuli but by internal factors. The surroundings and external events, which are considered external factors, may also influence a certain person's mood although the mood, itself is initiated by one's own mind state.

Mood affects a person's memory in two ways: mood congruence and mood dependence. Mood congruence happens when you remember memories that depict the mood you are currently feeling. For example, if you feel like you are in a bad mood, or more specifically feeling irritable at the moment, there is a possibility that you will be able to remember an event from the past where you also felt extremely annoyed by anyone or anything. This is what mood congruence means. The mood of the memory you retrieve is similar to the mood you are feeling during retrieval.

Mood dependence, on the other hand, affects both the encoding and retrieval phases. It suggests that recalling an event is easier when it was encoded under the same mood that you are currently having during retrieval. For example, when an information from the past was encoded in your brain during a happy moment, it will be easier to remember it when you are also feeling happy while retrieving it. The mood you had when you were encoding a memory is the same as the mood you are feeling during retrieval. To further clarify the subtle differences between the two effects, under the mood congruence, the mood during retrieval matches the mood of the memory, itself regardless how you were feeling while your brain was encoding it; while under the mood dependence, the mood during retrieval matches the mood during encoding regardless of the mood the memory being encoded is depicting.

Applying Emotions to Visuals

If only every information had emotional content attached to it, then you would be able to remember memories effortlessly. Sadly, things do not work that way. Extreme emotions are brought by reality and those emotionally-charged memories that stick forever to you only come from actual events. For you to remember the moments when you were still in love with someone, you have to experience the real feeling of "love" otherwise the mind will consider it as a temporary thought.

But come to think of it, there are a number of information that you need to retain not necessarily for a lifetime; but only for a rather lengthy period so you can store them in your mind at least until you actually use them. This just means you do not need to attain the realistic peaks of emotions. You just have to feel something less intense than reality but more realistic than imagination.

If the thoughts of hearing fingernails scrape a chalkboard gives you shiver, then you are more or less capable of feeling illusory emotions. You are going to need this ability to enhance your retention along with your visualization skill. Also, in applying emotions, remember that you need to be honest as much as possible. Focus on the realistic feeling you would get if the same thoughts happened in reality.

Let's start with a familiar example: Bryce the ostrich. What does he do again when he sees other birds flying? He cries. Imagine you are born as Bryce. You are so excited about your future because you think you'll be able to fly once you grow up. But day by day, you are starting to realize you are not meant to fly. You are not free as other birds. You live your whole life staying on the same ground and not being able to witness the beauty of the Earth from above.

How did you feel? Down? Frustrated? or Sympathetic? If what you felt was a feeling that is along the same lines, it means you have just projected a realistic emotion out of nothing but a thought. Because of that, you will now be able the remember Bryce every time you feel sad. The challenge in this application is combining the fanciful, exaggerated pictures with real, genuine emotions.

Now for a more comprehensive application, I need you to imagine the given scenario below and acquire all the feelings that will be mentioned. If you can pair each feeling with facial expression, then better.

Scenario:

It's Monday morning and you woke up realizing you're late for work again; so, you hurriedly took a bath, slipped into your uniform, and rushed into the office. When you entered the office, you noticed that some people were staring at you—at your face, to be specific. Some started laughing and others started calling you Mona Lisa. You felt embarrassed. You went into the bathroom to see what was wrong. Apparently, you forgot to put on eyebrows. You began freaking out that you couldn't even leave the bathroom because you were ashamed of your sparse eyebrows.

While still being undecided inside the bathroom, you started hearing horses neighing from outside. You opened the door in shock as there were already thousands of armored soldiers, some riding horses, who are killing each other. "It's the Crusades!" Your officemate shouted. You saw one of the soldiers coming to you but you couldn't move your legs. He was about to slash you until "boom!" your boss had shot him before his sword could reach you. "Ha! I saved you with my gun!" your annoying boss braggingly claimed. "I invented this gunpowder, myself! You better thank me and my ingenious gunpowder invention," he added. Although you were more annoyed than grateful as he had always been that boastful, still, you thanked him. Then he left and joined the intensifying clash once again.

You hid under one of those tables in the office trying not get nearly slashed again. The whole building was filled with sounds of swords slashing. While you were hiding from those crusaders, you saw a mischief of car-sized rats coming from your boss' office. "Eww!" You shrieked in pure disgust. The rats began biting the crusaders and spread infectious disease inside the room. While the leader of the giant rats was busy shouting "bubonic plague!", you managed to find your way out of the building.

Shortly after leaving the office, you started seeing another horde of horsemen from afar approaching your location. One of your officemates, running from the same direction, was shouting "Run! It's the Mongol invasion!" You were frightened by what you have heard. But what scared you the most is when you realized the soldiers riding the horses were actually zombies. You started running again for your life but this time, faster.

You went straight to a newspaper publisher and reported everything. However, one of the employees there told you that your report could not be published until after three days because the printing press had just been invented that day. You got so disappointed after knowing that your report cannot be published on the same day. Hoping for another chance, you went to another newspaper publisher. The firm also rejected your report because the news that it was going to release for that day was about the spread of Islam. You started becoming angry because you felt like these publishers were intentionally ignoring your report. "Why can't you prioritize my news!?" you furiously shouted as you walk out of the establishment.

On your way home, you heard a sound of flapping wings from above. It seemed to you that those were just a couple of birds flying around until you looked up and saw a flying... money? A flying money! A lot of paper bills with wings were flying above you. You immediately thought that they might be your chance to become a millionaire. So, you excitedly chased after them. You were too focused on them that you bumped into a tree. "Oh no!" you shouted, realizing you lost track of the flying paper bills. You didn't know on which direction you could find them again. You looked around and then you saw an old man holding his compass. You stared at his compass in envy thinking that you would have been able to chase those bills if you only had one. Losing your hope, you decided to just return home and you slept the rest of the day.

Did the story make sense to you? I guess it didn't. But congrats, you have just had a run-through of the nine important events that happened during the post-classical era in our world history. If you tried feeling the action in the story genuinely, then you can easily remember each of the event stated through associating it with the specific feeling you had. To sum up the emotions and the corresponding information each of them represents:

- Embarrassment - the creation of Mona Lisa during Renaissance period

- Surprise - the crusades: the battle between Christianity and Islam

- Annoyance - gunpowder invention

- Disgust - the pandemic: bubonic plague

- Fear - Mongol Invasion

- Disappointment - invention of printing press

- Anger - spread of Islam

- Excitement - Tang dynasty introduces the flying money

- Envy - the invention of the navigational tool: compass

CHAPTER 8

MIND MAPPING

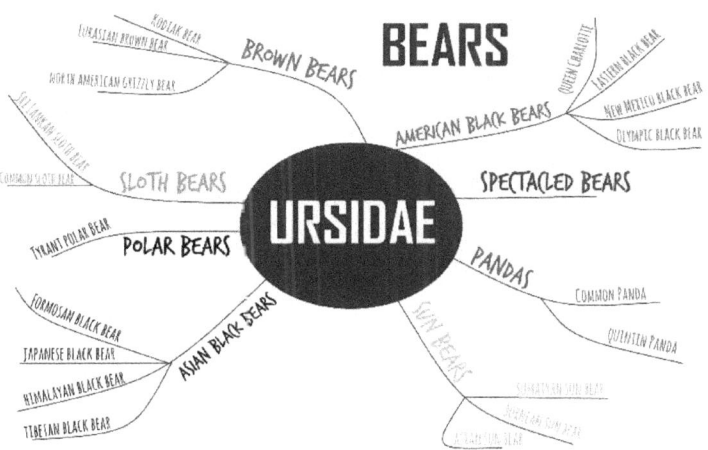

As you can see in the picture above, the details look like a bunch of stems sprouting from a seed in the center labeled as 'Ursidae." Ursidae is the family name for bears. But since it is a too general term, another set of information, sprouting from the center, is created to specify the species under the family Ursidae. Majority of the eight species of this family however, still cover subspecies under them that is why the second level of information further sprouts to another level to specify each species' subspecies—and that is what we call a mind map.

Mind mapping is a method of memorization that uses a chart-like organization of information or simply, a mind map. It is typically used to highlight the relationships among the information being memorized. Thus, it organizes information in a better and more understandable way. Moreover, in mind mapping, the mind focuses on the image of the map, itself and not necessarily on the image of each of the information included in it. For this reason, no mental image is needed to represent each particular item in the map although it is not a hard and fast rule. There are some who prefer using images for each information so they can imagine a map containing images instead of words. In such case, the use of linking method is advised.

Creating a Mind Map

To create a mind map, you need to start with identifying which among the information you have is the center information. The center information, from the name itself, will serve as the center of the mind map. It is the subject that encompasses all the other ideas that will be included in the map. The center information is usually the topic or theme of the details you need to memorize or the title of the lesson in which the details are discussed. In the picture above, the center information is the family name of the bears.

After identifying the center, you need to come up with a second level of information directly connected to the center. Classify all the other information based on how close they are to the center information. That way, you will know the number of main topics you have and understand their relationship to the center information. They either have a common relationship to the center information—like what we have on the picture above—or are separately related to the center information. Regardless of which, they are still going to be included in the second level as long as they are the nearest connectible topic to the center. In the sample mind map we have, the second level information, sprouting directly from the center, is composed of the species under the bear family. They have a common relationship to the center because they are all subspecies. Now if we have other information like history of bears, famous bears in the world, and non-government organizations for the welfare of bears, the second level of information will not anymore enumerate the species on the second level and will only include the collective topic "species of bear" instead. And in that case, notice that the new main topics namely, history of bears, famous bears in the world, organizations for bears, and species of bears do not anymore have a common relationship toward the center information. Nonetheless, they all are still considered the nearest topics to the center information and shall therefore compose the second level.

Now that you have a center information and main topics, you need to choose which among the information left are being described or covered by each of the main topics. Note that the rest of the information you have are all probably related to the main topics but you need to filter the information with the nearest connection from the ones which can still be included under another level. In the picture above, the set of branches sprouting from every second level branch comprises the subspecies of each species of the bear family. The third level is generally composed of subtopics.

If you still have pieces of information left, you can just create and connect another set of branches from the existing branches to provided places for each information. Do this until all the information you need are covered. Just make sure that each information really does have a relationship with the branch from which it sprouts so you can visualize a smooth flow of connection among the items in the mind map.

You can visualize a mind map directly in your mind or you can draw it to a piece of paper first and subsequently familiarize yourself with the flow. Also, a mind map does not have to be presented the same way as the picture above. You can organize the information in a simpler and neater way although I must emphasize again that the weirder the image, the longer it stays in the mind. If the branches on your mind map look exactly the same, chances are the memories may overlap during retrieval and may lead to you, forgetting some of the information. But still, retention is at optimum level when you memorize in a way that you and your mind prefer.

Analyzing a Mind Map

Knowing now how information flows in a mind map, we can now properly translate the sample picture. There are eight species under the family Ursidae namely, the brown bears, sloth bears, polar bears, Asian black bears, sun bears, pandas, spectacled bears, and American black bears. The second level further sprouts into third-level branches which means the majority of these species still cover a set of subspecies. Thus, we can say that the Kodiak bear, Eurasian brown bear, and North American grizzly bear are the subspecies of the species brown bears. The subspecies of sloth bears, on the other hand, are Sri Lankan sloth bear and the common sloth bear. Polar bears had a subspecies named tyrant polar bear—although take note that it is already considered extinct today. The Asian black bears' subspecies include, though not limited to, Formosan black bear, Japanese black bear, Himalayan black bear, and Tibetan black bear. Sun bears have Asian sun bear, Bornean sun bear, and Sumatran sun bear as its subspecies. Subspecies under the species panda or giant panda are common panda and Quintin panda. Spectacled bears ended on the second level for they have no subspecies. Lastly, the subspecies of the American black bears include, but not limited to, Olympic black bear, New Mexico black bear, eastern black bear, and the Queen Charlotte black bear.

Organize Your Own Mind Map

Let's try another challenge but this time, you're going to create your own mind map. We're also not discussing about bears—we're going to meet the gods and goddesses of the famous Greek mythology. Although we are not going to cover the overwhelming number of all Greek mythology characters, the names may still confuse you. So, try to analyze relationships and visualize the connections as you read each detail. You may draw the mind map on a piece of paper and follow the flow of relationships between these gods and goddesses or you may direct the visualization in your mind. The latter is more challenging and definitely more rewarding.

Starting with the first few greatest creations, Gaia, the personification of mother Earth, had a relationship with Uranus, the god of heavens. As a result of their love, twelve titans were born: Themis, the Titaness of divine law and order; Mnemosyne, the Titaness of memory; Hyperion, the titan of light; Theia, the Titaness of sight; Crius, the titan of constellations; Oceanus, the titan of the all-encircling river oceans; Tethys, the Titaness of fresh-water, Iapetus, the titan of mortality; Coeus, the titan of intellect; Phoebe, the Titaness of the prophecy; Cronus, the titan of harvests; and Rhea, the Titaness of fertility and motherhood. On the other hand, Aphrodite, the goddess of beauty and love was born through a sea foam from Uranus' genitals. It means she does not have any mother and the only parent she has is her father, Uranus.

Atlas, the titan who carried the heavens upon his shoulders was also born without a mother just like Aphrodite. He is the son of Iapetus. Oceanus and Tethys gave birth to Pleione, an Oceanid nymph. Coeus and Phoebe gave birth to Leto, the Titaness of motherhood. Cronus and Rhea, on the other hand, gave birth to the six renowned gods and goddesses: Zeus, the king of the gods, ruler of Mount Olympus, and the god of thunder; Hera, the queen of gods and the goddess of women; Poseidon, the god of the sea; Hestia, the virgin goddess of home; Hades, the god of the underworld and the dead; and Demeter, the goddess of harvest. Later on, Pleione and Atlas had an affair and resulted to the birth of Maia, the mother of Hermes.

Zeus, then began to produce his own children. He, and Semele gave birth to Dionysus. Zeus also had an affair with Maia who, as a result, gave birth to Hermes, the god of communication and trade. Zeus and Leto gave birth to the twin Olympians, Apollo and Artemis. Athena, the goddess of wisdom and battle strategy, also came from Zeus but without any mother. Lastly, Zeus and Hera gave birth to Ares, the god of war and violence, and Hephaestus, the god of metalworking and crafts.

You may now start drawing your own mind map. You may start by recalling the pieces of images you imagined while you were reading the story; and start organizing them based on relationships and sequence of existence. Form your own mind map and once you do, try to retell the story by yourself—then you'll know how helpful the mind map is.

CHAPTER 9

VISUALIZING NAMES

Getting to know a lot of people is all fun and games until you realize you cannot anymore remember all of their names. How can you? From your closest friends to the least noticed acquaintance, you are meant to know thousands of names in your life and it is impossible to remember all of them. You might be thinking that you are just not good at remembering people but actually, most of us feel the same thing too.

You might meet James Bond today or you might meet Nikolaj Coster-Waldau tomorrow. You really cannot know when a name is going to be easy and when it is going to be a burden. But cut the worries because one of the memorization techniques we have today are specifically developed to help people remember names. We'll call this technique as the connecting method since the bottom line of this method is to connect names with certain aspects. It is almost like the linking method except that we do not necessarily have a sequence of items to connect to each other but instead, we need to connect the information to itself. There are three bases to this method and any of which can be used to memorize names.

Appearance Connection

As you know, attention is significant in order to inject information in your mind. Your interest on someone instantly gives you the adequate amount of attention you need to be able to remember the name. If you try to pay the same level of attention to anybody, then you can possibly remember everyone's name. Appearance affects how much attention a person can provide that is why it is the first basis to the connecting method.

If you admire people because of their looks, chances are their names stick in your mind for a longer period. It is because you are fond of imagining their face at least once in a while that their names have been a part of your memory. If you ever had a crush on someone then you probably know what I'm talking about.

Come to think of it, even if you do not have personal interest or affection to some people, their names still stick in your memory because you can remember how these people appear. There are available mental images that correspond with the existence of the names in your mind; hence, you have both the names and the visuals. And that is actually the very point—you visualize.

If I introduce to you a person named Johnny Biggy, you'll probably forget about him just a few chapters after this exact moment. But if I describe him to you as a buff, blonde guy with curly hair who always wears a black leather coat and matches it with his funky metal earing on his right ear, you will be able to visualize him. Now the technique is, you do not need to force you brain to remember every description. Think about his surname "Biggy." Which among the descriptions I've given, may be linked or connected to such surname? The answer is his body figure. He's buff. You can label him in your mind as Johnny Biggy the buff. That way, you can remember him in an instant once you hear his name again.

Try to imagine a person named Jessica Bright as well. She's a woman of age 42 with a short hair who never forgets to apply sun screen to protect her white complexion. Now let's try to connect her name to the description. She's rich but it does not seem to have anything to do with her name. She's 42 but again, it has no impact to the mind. She has a white complexion. Now that's it. Her surname is Bright. Just imagine her shining so bright because of her white skin tone and most probably, you'll remember her for years.

Character Connection

Now what if Jessica Bright does not have a white complexion and she applies sun screen merely because she wants to protect her skin? You'll probably lose her name in an instant. However, if you find out that she's smart and holds a PhD in Mathematics, you will probably be able to remember her name again as Jessica is smart so she's bright; and therefore, she's Jessica Bright.

The next option you have on which you can base your memory of people's names is their traits and characteristics. If appearance can affect attention, a person's character can affect emotions. Do you remember the person whom you hated before? Don't deny it. We all have hated people before, most especially when we were still young and couldn't comprehend everything that other people did. Your hate, or basically any other feeling toward people is most probably influenced by their character. You admire smart people, get angry with bad people, and get happy when you are with funny people. You can easily remember the names of the people whose characters have had an impact to your life at least once.

The good news is that you don't have to meet and be with people every day just so you can remember their names. You just need to connect the traits they have with their names in any way possible. For example, the name Shawn Fury may not sound something your mind can remember for weeks. But if we connect it to one of his characteristics, then your mind might consider letting the name rest in your memory for a while. So, let's discuss about Shawn Fury. Shawn Fury is a head of a certain office's department. He is also smart like Jessica Bright although he's a slowpoke. He loves watching movies, playing chess, and yelling at his subordinates every time they do not meet his expectation. Also, he's rich and he fosters seventeen stray cats in his house. To connect, his first name Shawn does not really have a connection with any part of the description. But, his last name Fury has one—the fact that he loves yelling at his subordinates when they do not work the way he expects them to be. He is always angry so you can say he is Shawn "Furious" and your mind shall remember the name Shawn Fury.

Two-word names are actually easy to remember but unfortunately, that is not the common case. What if you meet someone whose name is Agatha Sherry Marie Routundder Smith? Don't panic. You should try to get to know her first. Agatha, despite his femininity, has a loud, deep voice. She loves performing on stage. In fact, she is a great dancer and theater actress. She always eats during class although she's clearly not that generous as she does not share her food no matter what. She also does not study much, perhaps because she is an active officer of one of their school's organization. With her active campus life, she often forgets about taking care of herself. She usually enters the room with a stained dress, or attends in class with her hair uncombed.

Among the given characteristics, which do you think will help you remember her name? If you do not have any answer nor a clue, then analyze how some of her characters are connected to her name. Agatha has a loud, deep voice and that can be represented by the sound of a thunderclap which is loud and deep as well. Notice that the fourth word in her name is Routundder. We can link the term "raw thunder" to it and make it sound like the actual pronunciation of the name Routundder. So, Agatha has a loud and deep voice that sounds like a raw thunder which also sounds like Routundder. Another characteristic that we can connect to Agatha is her messy habit of not grooming herself. She looks like she's working in a factory, or in a smithy. Yep, smithy as in her surname Smith. So, you can remember her by visualizing a girl named Agatha Sherry Marie with a voice of a Raw Thunder who works in a Smithy.

Meeting Place Connection

The meeting place is the most realistic basis among the three bases for connecting names to people.

Actual settings like park, school, supermarket, club, beach, and any other place can potentially trigger a memory that may depict either a scene or an image of a certain person. Meeting place connection does not require you to visualize a projected image because the place through which you can remember the person already exists. This technique is done by simply remembering the place where you met the specific person and associating it with the same person's name.

You've met Johnny Biggy, Jessica Bright, Shawn Fury, and Agatha Sherry Marie Routundder Smith in this book so you can say they are somehow counted. However, you may test your memory in a better way through a more realistic approach. You may speak of a certain place and observe if your mind can produce a name or names. The names that your mind will produce are most probably the names of the people whom you met or usually see in the stated place.

The bases you've learned are not strictly independent to each other. This means you can use a combination of any two or all to remember a person's name if that is what fits the situation the most. However, always bear in your mind that as much as possible, you need to single out the most practical basis among the three. If you can clearly remember a person's name through visualizing the place where you met that person, then do not struggle for connecting his name to another basis. No matter how large your memory is, if you do not know how to efficiently store information then its capacity will always seem so limited to you.

CHAPTER 10

VISUALIZING NUMBERS (MAJOR SYSTEM)

Most people find numbers as the hardest to memorize. Unlike letters, numbers cannot form words when combined nor form a mental image when read. Memorizing two to three digits is considerable while four to six digits are fine; but having to memorize seven to fifteen digits is punishing unless the digits are your own phone number. They can even form a 370-digit number and still be considered as a valid value. The thing is, numbers are infinite and that's what makes it confusing.

Major System

The pegs under the number rhyme and number shape systems replace the numbering on a certain list; thus, they, themselves represent numbers. For this reason, these systems are not your best choice for memorizing numbers since they may only lead to confusion. In such case, you may opt to use the major system. It is a peg system which replaces single-digit numeric values with sounds of letters or phonemes. Through it, any combination of numbers forming more than one digits will also be able to form different words and sounds.

0 = /s/ /z/ and /x/
1 = /t/ /d/ /θ/ and /ð/
2 = /n/
3 = /m/
4 = /r/
5 = /l/
6 = /ʃ/ /tʃ/ /dʒ/ /ʒ/
7 = /c/ /k/ hard g /q/
8 = /f/ /v/
9 = /p/ /b/

From the summarized list above, notice that each digit is represented by letters and symbols. So how is each letter or symbol connected to its corresponding digit? Let's start with zero (0). The easiest way to remember the letters for zero is through its first letter. Zero begins with the sound of *z* as in "zealous". Therefore, it also covers the sounds near to it like the sounds of *s* as in "snake" and *x* as in "xylophone".

The sounds associated with number one (1), on the other hand, is represented by letters written with a single vertical stroke each. Letters *t* and *d*, therefore, are the same with *1* which also only has one vertical stroke. The sounds of *t* as in "technique" and *d* as in "dog" are also relatively close to the sounds of *th* (θ) as in "thorn" and *th* (ð) as in "those." So, *th* (θ) and *th* (ð) are still included in the sounds and letters linked to number one.

The letters for numbers two to five are easier to remember. Two (2) is represented by *n* as in "night" because the letter *n* is written with two vertical strokes. Three (3), on the other hand, is represented by *m* as in "mammoth" as *m* contains three vertical strokes. Four (4) takes *r* as its symbol simply because it ends with the sound of *r* as in "rabbit." Five (5) is associated with *l* as in "Lamborghini" because in the system of Roman numeral, the number 50 is represented by L.

The number six (6) almost looks like the letter *G*, as well as the lower-case *g* when flipped both vertically and horizontally. Thus, six is the digit for the all the soft *g* sounds like gym and gesture. The sounds that are also covered by the number six are *j* (dʒ) as in "jump," *sh* (ʃ) as in "sure," *ch* (tʃ) as in "chimney," and the sound of *z* (ʒ) in "seizure."

The hard *g* sound like "goat" falls under the number seven (7). It also includes the sounds of *c* as in "caramel," *k* as in "karate," *q* as in "queue," and the sound of *ch* in "loch." Eight (8), on the other hand, covers the sounds of *f* and *ph* as in "free" and "phone." Sounds like *v* in "love" and *gh* in "laugh" also fall under the number eight.

To remember the letters and sounds for nine (9), just think of the letter *P* flipped horizontally or a lower-case *b* rotated 180°. The sounds of these letters, *p* as in "page" and *b* as in "baboon," are what represent the number nine. The vowels *a e i o u* and other consonants like *h y* and *w* are not assigned to any digit; hence, no value. They can be used to fill consonants to form a word without changing its value.

Usage

Using the summarized list, we can form any word that will make us remember the number to which it is linked. If I give you the word "hair" then you can tell it is a word for 4. The consonant *h* and the vowels *a* and *i* do not have any value but the letter *r* has. So, spelling out the letters in the word "hair" through their designated values, it is going to appear as 0004 or simply, 4. The word "owl" can be translated into 005 or 5 while the word "ham" is equal to 003 or 3.

Do not confuse the undesignated letters and sounds with those that represent the number zero. The word "may" is equivalent to 3-0-0, or when simplified becomes 3 while the word "max" may also be written as 3-0-0 but, when simplified, becomes 30. The two zeros in the word "may" come from the vowel *a* and consonant *y* which means they are not actual zeros and do not have any value under this system. However, only one of the two zeros in the word "max" has no value and it comes from the vowel *a*. X, on the other hand, is equal to an actual zero.

A word may also be formed containing two or more digits like "cheek" which is composed of ch-e-e-k or 6-0-0-7 or 67. "Metal" may be translated as 315. You can also form your own words by yourself using several combinations. For example, given the values 7 and 9 we can form words like cape or cope (7090) and pace (9070). Of course, if a value is composed of numbers in strict order, the choices will be limited. If we have 900941, the only single word we can form is "passport."

It is important to remember that unlike the other peg systems, the major system restricts the system to the given corresponding letters and sounds for each digit. So, you cannot change it based on what you prefer more. However, the words you can form through each digit or combination of digits are certainly up to you.

Sample words from 1-50:

1 tea (1-0-0 = 1)
2 hen (0-0-2 = 2)

3   ham (0-0-3 = 3)
4   ray (4-0-0 = 4)
5   wheel (0-0-0-0-5 = 5)
6   show (6-0-0 = 6)
7   hike (0-0-7-0 = 7)
8   wife (0-0-8-0 = 8)
9   wipe (0-0-9-0 = 9)
10 dose (1-0-0-0 = 10; again, do not confuse actual zeros with zeros that do not have value)
11 toad (1-0-0-1 = 11)
12 tune (1-0-2-0 = 12)
13 doom (1-0-0-3 = 13)
14 deer (1-0-0-4 = 14)
15 tool (1-0-0-5 = 15)
16 teach (1-0-0-6 = 16)
17 twice (1-0-0-7-0 = 17)
18 dive (1-0-8-0 = 18)
19 dub (1-0-9 = 19)
20 Nazi (2-0-0-0 = 20)
21 note (2-0-1-0 = 21)
22 neon (2-0-0-2 = 22)
23 enemy (0-2-0-3-0 = 23)
24 honor (0-0-2-0-4 = 24)
25 inhale (0-2-0-0-5-0 = 25)
26 nacho (2-0-6-0 = 26)

27 niece (2-0-0-7-0 = 27)
28 naive (2-0-0-8-0 = 28)
29 nap (2-0-9 = 29)
30 max (3-0-0 = 30)
31 meadow (3-0-0-1-0-0 = 31)
32 moon (3-0-0-2 = 32)
33 mime (3-0-3-0 = 33)
34 more (3-0-4-0 = 34)
35 mole (3-0-5-0 = 35)
36 mash (3-0-6 = 36)
37 mug (3-0-7 = 37)
38 movie (3-0-8-0-0 = 38)
39 mop (3-0-9 = 39)
40 erase (0-4-0-0-0 = 40)
41 road (4-0-0-1 = 41)
42 urine (4-0-0-2 = 42)
43 rum (4-0-3 = 43)
44 aurora (0-0-4-0-4-0 = 44)
45 royal (4-0-0-0-5 = 45)
46 rush (4-0-6 = 46)
47 rake (4-0-7-0 = 47)
48 wharf (0-0-0-4-8 = 48)
49 herb (0-0-4-9 = 49)
50 lazy (5-0-0-0 = 50)

Common Mistakes

Bear in mind that major system can lead to wrongful translations when not correctly used. The most common problem people commit when using this system is the addition of an extra sound to the word that is supposed to represent an exact combination of digits. So, you don't represent the number 17 with the word "duct" as it has an extra t sound at the end and therefore represents the number 171 (1+0+7+1).

Another common mistake is doubling the letter inside a word when not necessary. You cannot simply replace the word "diner" with "dinner" just because they both have the sound n in the middle. It can cause confusion as diner represents 124 (1+0+2+0+4) while dinner translates into 1224 (1+0+2+2+0+4). Refrain from doing such practice as it may lead to confusion most especially during exams.

Lastly, the most important thing to remember in major system is that it is about the sounds and not necessarily the letters. The word "place," when decoded shall result to 950 (9+5+n+0+n). The letter c takes the sound of s under the digit 0 and not the c under the digit 7. Thus, it should not be translated as 957 (9+5+n+7+n)

Notice that among all the memorization techniques, this system implements the strictest rules and specifications. But it is only because it prevents the confusion among the representations as confusion is exactly the problem why numbers are hard to memorize. Still, the major system is the greatest tool you can use when it comes to dealing with numbers.

CHAPTER 11

VISUALIZING NUMBERS (OTHER SYSTEMS)

The major system is generally the best choice when it comes to memorizing any given set of numbers. However, if you cannot find your way yet to master the major system technique, you may choose to settle first with other less extensive, but almost as effective, techniques of dealing with numbers. Although it is the major system that can dramatically improve your flexibility in memorizing numbers, it will be best for you if you first try the simpler methods and then just work your way to mastering the major system. Methods like chunking and the PAO system adopt less strict rules to simplify the process of memorization.

Chunking System

The easiest way to remember a set of various digits is through chunking. It is basically dividing a long number into chunks of either two, three, or four digits, to remember the set as a collection of groups of numbers and not as a single group of many digits. You may have noticed before that your phone number, PIN number, and other important numbers are presented with divisions or groupings. It is actually an example of chunking. It doesn't just divide numbers. It makes the numbers look more organized and therefore easier to remember.

For example, you need to memorize the number 343189563231. Just by looking at it, your eyes might already be hurting. To avoid the feeling of getting overwhelmed by a 12-digit number, let's try chunking it into six groups:

34-31-89-56-32-31

Through chunking, you can now read it as thirty-four, thirty-one, eighty-nine, fifty-six, thirty-two, and thirty-one. Thus, chunking also makes the number easier to read and pronounce. However, grouping the digits by twos may not be practical most especially when you are given a longer set. Therefore, let's try to chunk it into four groups:

343-189-563-231

You may memorize it now as three hundred forty-three, one hundred eighty-nine, five hundred sixty-three, and two hundred thirty-one. Observe that the terms from translating number into words may have lengthen a bit but they are actually fewer this time. If under the six-group chunks you read six separate numbers, in here you read only four separate numbers. If you want to make it less, you can divide the set into three chunks:

3431-8956-3231

So, it is now read as three thousand four hundred thirty-one, eight thousand nine hundred fifty-six, three thousand two hundred thirty-one. The number of digits in a chunk typically ranges from one to four. Five or more chunks may already lose the sense of chunking since they still seem a bulk of unmemorizable number. Also remember that as much as possible, start the division from the last digits so the first chunk will contain the least number of digits in case there is uneven distribution. To demonstrate, you are given the 11-digit password 20685485471. You cannot evenly distribute the numbers into chunks of two, three, nor four. So, if you decide to use the four-digit chunks, it shall be rewritten as 206-8548-5471.

Decoding Chunks using Major System

To practice the application of the major system on the chunking method, let's try to decipher a long set of numbers. At this point, we can now apply both the chunking method and the major system to decipher numbers that are composed of a lot of digits. You may divide the digits into a certain number of chunks depending on your preference. Let's use this 20-digit passcode as an example:

13219540947001886751

Distributing the set into two-digit chunks, you'll get:

13-21-95-40-94-70-01-88-67-51

After chunking, assign a word to each chunk using the representational codes under the major system.

Make sure that what you assign to a single chunk is also a single word as much as possible as assigning more than two words to a single chunk does not sound practical. Besides, you are chunking to make memorization easier and not to memorize longer sentences. To help you form and assign words, presented below is the major system's summary of codes:

0 = /s/ /z/ and /x/
1 = /t/ /d/ /θ/ and /ð/
2 = /n/
3 = /m/
4 = /r/
5 = /l/
6 = /ʃ/ /tʃ/ /dʒ/ /ʒ/
7 = /c/ /k/ hard g /q/
8 = /f/ /v/
9 = /p/ /b/

Now let's try to make words out of the chunks we have:

13 - team
21 - neat
95 - blue

40 - horse
94 - pair
70 - case
01 - haste
88 - off
67 - jog
51 - late

You may just memorize the sequence of words assigned to the chunks although if you want to make things easier, you may visualize a scenario covering all the words assigned in sequence. Let's say, your team is not color blue and the horse is not your pair. In your case, you must haste to jump off and jog because you're late. The scene created honestly sounds weird but your mind can easily remember it; hence, it makes the number easy to remember.

Notice, however, that the sentence is quite long to memorize. So, let's try to chunk the set again but this time, we chunk it by threes:

13-219-540-947-001-886-751

Assigning words to each chunk we have: doom is when your honeydew lawyers brook the sixth huffish cloud. Remember, your first word represents only two-digit numbers since the first chunk always gets the least number of digits in case the set is not distributable evenly; so, get used to it. If you feel like you can get a simple and easier sentence, then you may distribute the set into four-digit chunks:

1321-9540-9470-0188-6751

Dominate the players because they practice all stuff with chocolate. A sentence that is as simple as that can already make you remember a 20-digit passcode. Therefore, chunks of three digits or four digits are more convenient and efficient to use.

PAO System

The combination of chunking and major systems actually explains how the PAO system works. PAO is an acronym that stands for Person-Action-Object system. It's a systematic way of forming a sentence that is literally composed of a person, an action, and an object. Through this technique, visualization of a single scenario that exhibits exactly what the sentence explains, can already make you remember a combination of six digits.

Like the major system, PAO system works best if you create your preliminary list of pegs although PAO is composed of not only one, but three sets of lists. You should also understand that PAO uses the same set of representational codes coming from other systems—in this case, from the major system. To demonstrate, consider the sample list of pegs below:

Number	Person	Action	Object
21	Nath	note	nut
40	Rose	hears	horse
58	Lovey	leave	loaf

From the list above, we can say that Nath note the nut is a sentence for number 21. Notice that it doesn't have to follow the strict grammar rules as it may alter the words and result to confusion. 40, on the other hand, may be translate into Rose hears the horse and 58 may be remembered as Lovey leave the loaf.

If you need to chunk a long number, make sure that each chunk consists the same number of digits as what you have on your list. Since the pegs above represent two-digit numbers, you need to divide a long number into chunks of two digits. If you have 405821, then you should divide it as 40-58-21. Now how is PAO system applied here?

The first chunk takes the person peg; so, the number 40 takes the name Rose. The second chunk takes the action; thus, 58 takes the action hears. The third chunk then takes the object; so, 21 takes the object nut. To translate 405821, we can use the sentence, "Rose hears the nut."

If your number is composed of more than six digits, you need to divide the number first into groups of six before diving each group into chunks of two. That means if you have 309845317234, you have to rewrite it as 30-98-45 and 31-72-34. In such case, you need to memorize two sentences to memorize the digits.

CHAPTER 12

MEMORY PALACE

For centuries, mnemonists claim the palace method as the greatest memorization technique. It is also called the loci or the journey method as it somehow allows the user to "journey" through his memory storage. Renowned for its dramatic effects on the memory, people up until this age utilize the use of this technique to memorize almost anything. But how does the palace method exactly work?

The palace method uses a virtual storage called the memory palace. The memory palace is any place or structure that serves as a storage of information. It only exists in the mind and can take any form of structure such as a house, an office, a market, or anything. It can be as small as a closet or as huge as an actual palace. It can be as simple as a room or as complex as a maze. It can also take the form of an existing place. As a matter of fact, a lot of mnemonists use their own houses as their memory palace.

The purpose of the memory palace is to provide a space through which a person can travel and retrieve his memory. Yes, you can virtually travel through the memory palace and consciously retrieve memories from it. It's like a locker where you can safekeep your things and get them whenever they are needed, except that it's a large, walk-in locker. You can place any information in the form of a mental image at a specific place or position inside the memory palace. Visualizing and connecting the mental image to its place or position will ease the retrieval of the information.

Scenario:

I'm going to describe a place and I need you to visualize every detail clearly as we are going to enter a room. On the doorstep is a brown, dusty doormat that says "please leave your shoes there," with an arrow pointing on the left, where the shoe rack is located. The entrance is not that wide but is enough to allow two people to enter. Three steps from the door, on the left is a small bathroom. Walking further, there is a red, medium-sized sofa facing the television set. Immediately at the right of the sofa is a wooden study desk with three drawers below and a small lampshade on it. Between the sofa and the tv is a glass table on a golden-brown carpet. Next to the tv set, on its left, stands an old, dirty white refrigerator and just beside it is the sink. That's it. You've just had a tour around a memory palace.

Designing Your Own Memory Palace

Structure Memory palace is not just an empty room where you can dump information and retrieve them. It has to have details. It has to both look and feel real. Now you might be thinking that creating a memory palace is just an additional burden to memorize. Well, actually, the thing you need to remember in constructing your memory palace is familiarity.

The reason a lot of mnemonists use their own house is because they are already familiar with it. There's no memorization needed. You just have to visualize your own house. If you don't want to use your house, then make sure that the place you are going to use as a memory palace should be, as much as possible, a place you are very familiar to.

Size
The size of the palace also matters. It has to be spacious enough so you can feel like you are indeed, travelling. It should not be too narrow but it shouldn't also be too wide. If the place is too narrow, it means you cannot walk around it. If it's too wide, then that means the place seems empty and you are not maximizing the space available. Just make sure you can "walk around" the place and that shall be enough.

Complexity
The complexity, on the other hand, plays an important role in the capacity of the memory palace. Details, in the form of furniture, appliances, or designs in the house should be realistic as they are the specific places or positions in which you can put

information. The directions, on the other hand, should not in any case add to your confusion. The sections, divisions, and directions within the structure should allow you to navigate the place freely. It doesn't matter if the memory palace is as complex as a maze. As long as you are familiar to it and you can travel around without getting lost, that's completely fine.

The reason you have to regard the familiarity of structure, spaciousness of size, and the level of complexity when it comes to building a memory palace is that they make "navigating" the mind easy. Notice that we are using words like walk, travel, and navigate as if we are talking about an actual place; but as far as the palace method is concerned, these words simply mean to think of or to recall a memory. To further understand how memory palace works, let's try to encode the list below:

Party Foods:

- pizza
- red wine

- buffalo wings
- burger
- popcorn
- chicken nuggets
- cake
- brownies
- ribs
- fries
- lasagna
- bacon strips
- cookies
- soda

Since, most probably you haven't designed your own memory palace yet, let's just use the room that was previously described. Entering the room, the first detail we can use as a specific storage for a single information is the brown, dusty doormat. To connect both the place and information, you can imagine the doormat is a one, rectangular slice of pizza. The next detail available shall be the shoe rack so imagine the shoe rack containing red wines tied with shoe laces instead of ribbons. Walking in, imagine you hear a buffalo singing inside the bathroom as you pass by it. That shall connect the buffalo wings to the bathroom.

Now, imagine the sofa as a huge burger and the show on tv is about producing popcorn. Also picture a chicken sitting on the study desk (chicken nuggets) staring at the cake beside it. Imagine the cake having a birthday lampshade on it instead of a candle. Since the desk has three drawers, we can use these drawers to place a total of three information. Imagine the pull or knob of the top drawer is colored brown (brownies). The second one's knob, on the other hand, is a bone (ribs) while that of the third drawer is made of potato (fries).

Replace the glass table with a huge lasagna and the carpet with large bacon strips. After then, imagine the ref's door bombarded with cookie magnets. Lastly, imagine the faucet on the sink producing soda instead of water.

After you placing each information in its place, try to imagine reentering the room and see if you can retrieve all the items. If you can, then that means you did the palace method correctly. If you cannot recall all the scenarios, just keep on practicing. Remember, the palace method does not rely heavily on the retrieval process; as it is all about the encoding of information. Make sure that you place information in specified details and that you visualize each connection properly.

Random Pick Up

To prove the flexibility of this method, try to answer the following questions based on the set of information we've just placed:

- The singing you hear from the bathroom every time you walk past it represents what food?

- What does the faucet on the sink produce?

- The lampshade is on what food?

- The table was replaced by what food?

- What does the show on tv represent?

If you have answered all the questions just by reimagining the memory palace, then you have just proven the method's flexibility. Using the memory palace, you can retrieve information properly even without recalling the sequence. Like when you were asked what the faucet produces, you can certainly proceed to where the sink is placed, and immediately connect the faucet with soda. In other words, you can remember the soda without first reciting all the other things on the list that come before it.

Memory palace does not just help you visualize information. Is also helps expand your retention capacity. You also get to enjoy the feeling of being able to "travel" inside your memory. Keep on practicing this method and for sure, you will master memorization eventually.

CONCLUSION

From all the tricks and techniques you have learned, we can now redefine photographic memory as the ability to consistently use visualization to form memory visuals through the use of various techniques and methods.

That definitely sounds more realistic and achievable. However, you should remember that regardless of how you define it, the most important thing is that you have learned the techniques to improve your memory. After all, these techniques are your true achievement.

You are now aware of the link or linking system which is best for memorizing details in order. You are now also knowledgeable with the peg systems covering the number rhyme, number shape, and the alphabet peg systems; as well as the major and PAO systems that are specially developed to memorize numbers. Also, you now know about the emotion-based system wherein you can also practice connecting your feelings to your visuals.

If you love organizing information before memorizing them, then you may now opt to use the mind map method. To remember names, you can now apply the connecting method. And above all, to memorize any kind and any set of information, you now know where to go—the memory palace.

All these techniques that you have learned, when frequently used, will not only improve your speed in memorizing information but will also expand your memory. Having a great memory is not a matter of birth, but a matter of hard work. So, keep on practicing! And in case you're wondering where to start, remember that long number you skipped in the introduction? Try decoding it using the major system.

Good luck!

P.S. Don't forget to grab a copy of your Free Bonus book "*How to Talk to Anyone: 50 Best Tips and Tricks to Build Instant Rapport*". If you want to increase your influence and become more effective in your conversations then this book is for you.

Just go to

http://ryanjames.successpublishing.club/freebonus/

Thank you!

Before you go, I just wanted to say thank you for purchasing my book.

You could have picked from dozens of other books on the same topic but you took a chance and chose this one.

So, a HUGE thanks to you for getting this book and for reading all the way to the end.

Now I wanted to ask you for a small favor. **Could you please take just a few minutes to leave a review for this book?**

This feedback will help me continue to write the type of books that will help you get the results you want. So if you enjoyed it, please let me know! (-:

www.ingramcontent.com/pod-product-compliance
Lightning Source LLC
Chambersburg PA
CBHW071721020426
42333CB00017B/2346